Why do we remember?

GUY FAWKES AND THE GUNPOWDER PLOT

Izzi Howell

W
FRANKLIN WATTS
LONDON • SYDNEY

Franklin Watts
First published in Great Britain in 2016 by The Watts Publishing Group
Copyright © The Watts Publishing Group, 2016

Produced for Franklin Watts by
White-Thomson Publishing Ltd
www.wtpub.co.uk

HB ISBN: 978 1 4451 4850 2
PB ISBN: 978 1 4451 4852 6

Credits:
Series Editor: Izzi Howell
Series Designer: Rocket Design (East Anglia) Ltd
Consultant: Philip Parker

The publisher would like to thank the following for permission to reproduce their pictures: Alamy/The Print Collector 4; Alamy/UrbanImages 7; Alamy/Mary Evans Picture Library 10; Alamy/Archivist 14–15; Alamy/StockyStoc 29; iStock/Linda Steward cover (background) and title page; iStock/golibo 2, 11 (left), 16 (top), 18, 20, 21, 22 and 25; iStock/TonyBaggett/coloured by Tim Mayer cover (front), 12–13 and 28; iStock/Duncan1890 6 (all) and 16 (bottom); iStock/claudiodivizia 23 (bottom); Mary Evans/Everett Collection 17; Mary Evans Picture Library 19; Mary Evans/Illustrated London News Ltd 26; Shutterstock/kishivan title page (bottom); Shutterstock/Avis De Miranda 3; Shutterstock/LianeM 5; Shutterstock/Everett Historical 8 and 9; Shutterstock/D Russell 78 11 (right); Shutterstock/Liubov Terletska 15; Shutterstock/Fedor Sefivanov 23 (top); Shutterstock/amir bajrich 24; Shutterstock/Kiev.Victor 27.
All design elements from Shutterstock.

Every attempt has been made to clear copyright. Should there be any inadvertent omission please apply to the publisher for rectification.

Printed in China

MIX
Paper from
responsible sources
FSC® C104740

Franklin Watts
An imprint of
Hachette Children's Group
Part of The Watts Publishing Group
Carmelite House
50 Victoria Embankment
London EC4Y 0DZ

An Hachette UK Company
www.hachette.co.uk
www.franklinwatts.co.uk

Words in **bold** can be found in the glossary on p30.

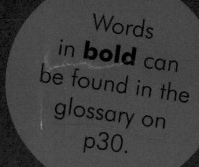

Some quotes have been simplified and revised with modern spelling

CONTENTS

WHAT WAS THE GUNPOWDER PLOT?

In 1605, a group of **Catholic** men planned to kill the **Protestant** king of England, King James I (1566–1625), by blowing up the **Houses of Parliament** with **gunpowder**.

They knew the king would be in Parliament on 5 November, so they chose that day for the explosion. This plan is known as the Gunpowder Plot.

▶ On the night of 4 November, two men found a member of the plot with gunpowder under the Houses of Parliament.

HOW do we know?

Poems can help us to remember important events from the past. This poem about the Gunpowder Plot was written in the 19th **century**.

WHAT do you think?

Do you think that this poem helps people to learn about the Gunpowder Plot? Why or why not?

▼ Today, people light bonfires on 5 November to remember the events of the Gunpowder Plot.

Remember, remember, the fifth of November,

Gunpowder, **treason** and plot.

We see no reason, why gunpowder treason

Should ever be forgot.

CATHOLICS <u>AND</u> PROTESTANTS

During the 16th century, there were many religious changes in England. King Henry VIII wanted to **divorce** his wife, Catherine of Aragon, but he wasn't allowed to by the Catholic Church. Henry VIII started his own Protestant Church, called the Church of England, which allowed him to divorce Catherine and marry Anne Boleyn instead.

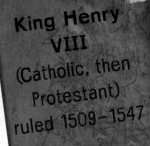

King Henry VIII
(Catholic, then Protestant)
ruled 1509–1547

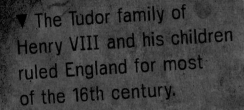

▼ The Tudor family of Henry VIII and his children ruled England for most of the 16th century.

King Edward VI
(Protestant)
ruled 1547–1553

Queen Mary I
(Catholic)
ruled 1553–1558

Queen Elizabeth I
(Protestant)
ruled 1558–1603

After Henry VIII's death, England went back and forth between being a Protestant country and a Catholic country, depending on the ruler. When England was a Catholic country, Protestants were treated badly. Many were killed because they would not become Catholics. Catholics were also treated badly by Protestant rulers.

FIND OUT FOR YOURSELF
Who was the first Tudor king?

<u>HOW</u> do we know?

We can see **memorials** to people who were killed because they would not change their religion in the 16th century. These people are known as **martyrs**.

DERYK CARVER
FIRST PROTESTANT MARTYR
BURNT AT LEWES. JULY 22ND 1555.
LIVED IN THIS BREWERY.

RECONSTRUCTED 1974

◄ This sign marks the place where a Protestant martyr lived.

A NEW KING

Henry VIII's daughter, Queen Elizabeth I, didn't have any children. When she died in 1603, King James VI of Scotland became the king of England (where he ruled as King James I). James was a Protestant, but his mother had been Catholic, so English Catholics hoped that he would treat them well.

► King James had been the king of Scotland for over thirty years when he became the king of England and Scotland in 1603.

WHAT do you think?

Which items in this picture show us that James I was a rich king?

I am
" an old and
experienced king."
King James I of England

However, life for Catholics in England didn't get better under James I. The powerful English **Members of Parliament** passed a **law** that Catholics had to go to Protestant churches. Many Catholics didn't want to go to Protestant churches and **worshipped** at home in secret.

▼ King James I talking to the English Parliament in London

FIND OUT FOR YOURSELF
What was the name of James' mother?

Shhh! I'm talking now!

CATESBY AND FAWKES

Robert Catesby was born in 1572 to an English Catholic family. His father went to prison several times because the Catesby family didn't go to Protestant church services. Catesby felt angry about the way his family had been treated. He started to plan the Gunpowder Plot, but he couldn't do it alone.

Come on guys, I need your help!

WHAT do you think?

Why do you think that Catesby needed people to help him with the Gunpowder Plot?

◀ Robert Catesby

Guy Fawkes was born in 1570 to an English Protestant family. After Guy's father died in 1578, his mother married a Catholic man and the family became Catholic.

Guy Fawkes was a passionate Catholic. At about the age of 21, he travelled to Europe to fight with the Catholic Spanish Army. Later, Fawkes asked the Spanish king, Philip III, to help English Catholics take control of England, but Philip said no.

How can I make England Catholic?

◄ Guy Fawkes was also known as Guido – the Spanish name for 'Guy'.

▲ Guy Fawkes learned how to use gunpowder while he was fighting in the Spanish Army.

MORE MEMBERS

In 1604, Robert Catesby started to look for Catholic men to help him with the Gunpowder Plot. Catesby was **charismatic**, so it was easy for him to **persuade** other people to join him.

"His conversation and manners were peculiarly attractive ... he had an irresistible influence over those who knew him."

Father Tesimond, speaking about Robert Catesby in the book he wrote about the Gunpowder Plot

▼ This drawing shows eight of the 13 main members of the Gunpowder Plot.

Christopher Wright

John Wright

Thomas Bates

Robert Wintour

Thomas Percy

Catesby looked for people who had useful skills, such as Guy Fawkes, who could use gunpowder. Catesby also **recruited** Thomas Percy, who knew important people at Parliament, and his cousins, Thomas and Robert Wintour.

The plotters decided that they would make King James I's daughter, Elizabeth, queen of England after the explosion. As she was only nine, they thought they could persuade her to become a Catholic.

Robert Catesby

Guy Fawkes

Thomas Wintour

WHAT do you think?

Why do you think that the members of the Gunpowder Plot decided to take part, even though they knew it would be dangerous?

THE HOUSES OF PARLIAMENT

In 1605, the Houses of Parliament were made up of many small buildings. The plotters planned to blow up a part known as the House of Lords. This is where a special **ceremony** to celebrate the first meeting of Parliament that year would take place on 3 October 1605.

HOW do we know?

We can see what the Houses of Parliament looked like at the time of the Gunpowder Plot by looking at drawings and paintings. These buildings burned down in a fire in 1834.

▼ This drawing shows what the Houses of Parliament looked like in 1605.

House of Lords

Houses of Parliament

WHAT do you think?

What differences can you see between the old Houses of Parliament and the Houses of Parliament today?

▶ The modern Houses of Parliament were rebuilt after the fire of 1834.

Westminster Abbey

Westminster Abbey

Houses of Parliament

FIND OUT FOR YOURSELF
What is Big Ben in the modern Houses of Parliament?

PLANNING, PLOTTING AND PLAGUE

In March 1605, the plotters rented a cellar under the Houses of Parliament. Over the next few months, they secretly brought barrels of gunpowder to the cellar and hid them under pieces of wood.

▲ Some people think that the members of the Gunpowder Plot transported the barrels of gunpowder to the cellar along the River Thames.

◄ Guy Fawkes helped to hide the gunpowder barrels.

During the summer of 1605, many people in London were worried about an **infectious** disease called the **plague**. Members of Parliament didn't want to come to London in case they became ill. They decided not to meet until 5 November 1605. The Gunpowder Plot would have to wait.

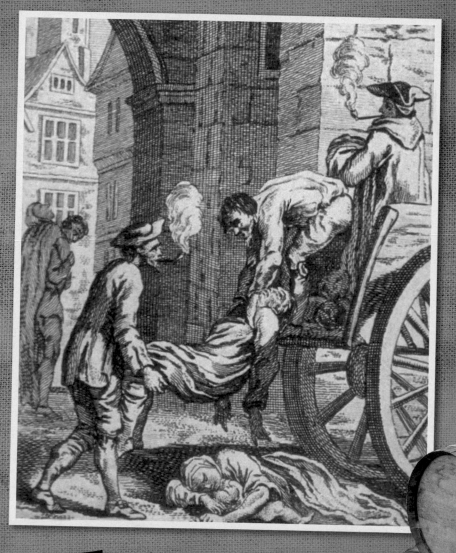

◀ There were several **outbreaks** of plague in London in the 17th century. Each time, horse-drawn carts drove around the city to collect the dead bodies.

WHAT do you think?

How do you think the plotters felt while they were waiting?

A MYSTERIOUS LETTER

On 26 October 1605, an **anonymous** letter was sent to Lord Monteagle, a Catholic Member of Parliament. The letter warned him to stay away from Parliament on 5 November because something bad was going to happen. The king was told about the letter, but at first, the **government** decided not to act.

Catesby **accused** the plotter Francis Tresham of sending the letter because Tresham was Lord Monteagle's **brother-in-law** and would have wanted to keep him safe. However, Tresham said that it didn't come from him. As the government didn't seem worried by the letter, the plotters decided to go ahead with their plans.

It wasn't me though!

▶ Catesby accusing Tresham of sending the letter to Lord Monteagle.

HOW do we know?

We can read the letter sent to Lord Monteagle.

"My Lord...I would advise you as you tender (value) your life to devise (come up with) some excuse to shift your attendance at this Parliament."

▲ The letter that was sent to Lord Monteagle, warning him to stay away from Parliament.

WHAT do you think?

Why do you think that the letter was sent anonymously?

CAUGHT IN THE CELLAR

On the evening of 4 November, Guy Fawkes went to the cellar under the Houses of Parliament to prepare the gunpowder so that it would be ready for the next day.

◀ Guy Fawkes was chosen to prepare the gunpowder because he had used it before.

FIND OUT FOR YOURSELF
How many barrels of gunpowder were hidden in the cellar?

At that same time, a group of men was searching the rooms under the Houses of Parliament to make sure that the building was safe for the ceremony on 5 November. They found Guy Fawkes with the gunpowder in the cellar and arrested him.

▶ Guy Fawkes' arrest

WHAT
do you think?

How do you think Guy Fawkes felt after the Gunpowder Plot was discovered?
How do you think the Members of Parliament felt?

GUY FAWKES SPEAKS

After his arrest, Guy Fawkes was taken to King James I. He told him that he was planning to blow up the Houses of Parliament, but he wouldn't tell the king his real name or the names of the other plotters.

▶ Guy Fawkes told the king that his name was John Johnson.

I'm not telling!

WHAT do you think?

Why didn't Guy Fawkes tell the king the truth about the Gunpowder Plot?

On 6 November, Guy Fawkes was taken to the prison in the Tower of London. He was **tortured** for three days until he told the guards his real name and the names of the other plotters. He admitted what they had been planning to do.

▼ Guy Fawkes was brought to the Tower of London by boat. He was taken into the building through a gate called Traitor's Gate.

Traitor's Gate

HOW do we know?

You can visit the Tower of London and see Traitor's Gate.

▶ Traitor's Gate is an entrance for boats.

THE END OF THE PLOT

When the other plotters found out that Guy Fawkes had been arrested, they escaped to the countryside. They hid at the homes of other Catholics that they knew.

On 8 November, a **sheriff** and his men found most of the escaped plotters. When the plotters fought the sheriff, some plotters, including Catesby, were killed. The sheriff arrested the other plotters, including Thomas Wintour, and took them to London.

WHAT do you think?

Why do you think the members of the plot fought back against the sheriff?

FIND OUT FOR YOURSELF
Which two members of the plot were killed by the same bullet?

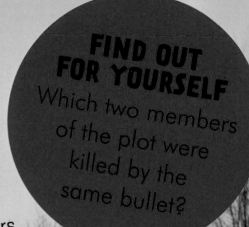

◄ Most members of the plot escaped from London on horseback.

After a **trial**, the remaining members of the Gunpowder Plot, including Guy Fawkes, were found guilty. They were **executed** in January 1606.

Guy Fawkes

▲ The execution of Guy Fawkes took place outside the Houses of Parliament.

AFTER THE GUNPOWDER PLOT

Life for Catholics in England became even harder after the Gunpowder Plot was discovered. Even though only a few Catholics were part of the plot, Protestants were **suspicious** of all Catholics and treated them badly for many years.

It wasn't until the late 18th century that Catholics started to be treated the same as Protestants in England. In England today, there are laws that say that everyone must be treated the same, no matter what their religion.

▼ This drawing shows a protest held by angry Protestants when Catholics were given the same **rights** as them in the 19th century, such as owning land.

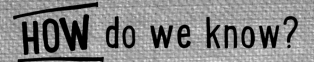 HOW do we know?

Today, you can see Catholic churches and celebrations in towns and cities across England.

▲ Westminster Cathedral is the biggest Catholic church in England. It opened in 1903.

WHAT do you think?

What types of religious building can you see in your neighbourhood?

REMEMBER, REMEMBER

Up until 1859, Protestant churches held services every year on 5 November to remember the plot and celebrate its failure.

From the late 19th century, children made models of Guy Fawkes out of old clothes. They would take them out on to the streets and ask for money by shouting 'a penny for the Guy'. Later, the model would be burned on a bonfire.

▼ These boys have added a barrel of 'gunpowder' to their Guy (model of Guy Fawkes).

Today, people across the UK celebrate 5 November with firework displays and bonfires. For this reason, 5 November is often known as Bonfire Night.

HOW do we know?

You can visit a Bonfire Night celebration in your local area.

◀ This huge model of Guy Fawkes will be burnt on a bonfire as part of the Bonfire Night celebrations in the town of Lewes.

WHAT do you think?

Why will you remember the story of the Gunpowder Plot?

GLOSSARY

accuse – to say that someone has done something bad

anonymous – describes something that was made or done by an unknown person

brother-in-law – the husband of your sibling or the brother of your husband or wife

Catholic – someone who belongs to a branch of the Christian religion that has the Pope as its leader

century – a period of a hundred years. The 16th century begins in 1500 and ends in 1599.

ceremony – a formal event

charismatic – describes someone whom other people want to please and be around

divorce – to stop being married to someone

executed – to be killed by someone else legally

government – the group of people that are in charge of a country

gunpowder – a powder that explodes when you set it on fire

Houses of Parliament – the buildings where the people who are elected to make laws do their work

infectious – describes a disease that can be easily passed from person to person

law – one of the rules of a country

martyr – a person who is killed because of their religion

Member of Parliament – someone who is elected to make laws for a country

memorial – a statue or sign put up to remind people of an event from the past

outbreak – when something unwanted, such as a war or a disease, suddenly happens

persuade – to make someone want to do something by talking to them about it

plague – a terrible disease that killed a lot of people in the past

Protestant – someone who belongs to the branch of the Christian religion that split from the Catholic Church in the 16th century

recruit – to try to persuade someone to work with you

rights – something that the laws of your country allow you to do

sheriff – in the past, sheriffs acted as policemen and worked to keep the land safe for the king

suspicious – describes someone who doesn't trust another person

torture – to hurt someone to try to make them tell you something

treason – the crime of doing something to hurt your country, ruler or government

trial – a meeting in which people decide if someone is guilty of a crime

worship – to take part in a religious ceremony

TIMELINE

1534	Henry VIII stops being a Catholic and founds the Protestant Church of England.
1570s	Guy Fawkes and Robert Catesby are born.
1603	Elizabeth I dies. James I becomes the king of England.
1604	Catesby starts to recruit people for the plot.
March 1605	The plotters rent a cellar under the Houses of Parliament.
4 Nov 1605	Guy Fawkes is caught and arrested.
6 Nov 1605	Guy Fawkes is tortured until he confesses.
8 Nov 1605	Most of the remaining plotters are arrested.
Jan 1606	Guy Fawkes and many other plotters are executed in London.
late 18th and 19th centuries	Catholics are gradually given the same rights as Protestants in England.

FIND OUT FOR YOURSELF ANSWERS

p7 – Henry VII. p9 – Mary, Queen of Scots.
p15 – Big Ben is the bell in the clock tower
in the Houses of Parliament.
p20 – Thirty six.
p24 – Robert Catesby and Thomas Percy.